First Printing, 2018

Goodbye, Summer!
You'll be missed.
You have been so cool.
But, now it's time to change my gears
and prepare for
back to school.

New haircuts and new outfits
with brand new
clothes and shoes,
will help me to avoid the hated
end-of-summer blues.

I have my list,
now to the store
for all my school supplies.
A binder and a new notebook
will help me organize.

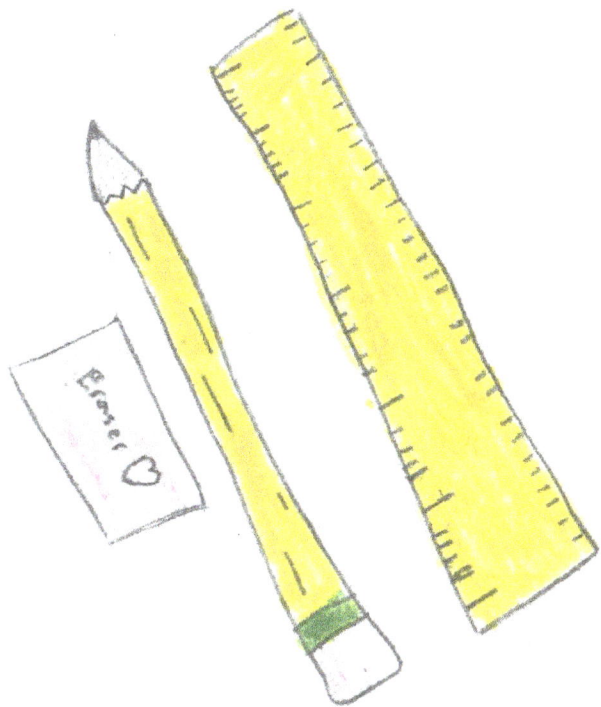

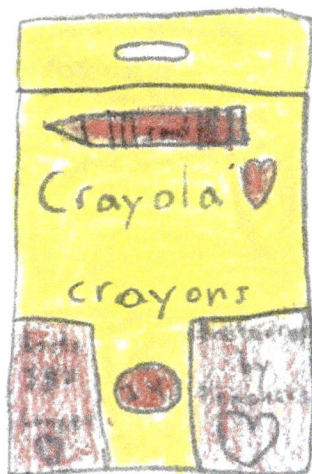

Sharpened pencils,
crisp papers,
folders,
pens, and
crayons…
I'll be all packed and ready
for new school year
goals and plans.

Back to school
means seeing friends
that I have missed all summer.
Some will be in different classes,
and that will be a bummer.

But I will meet some new friends
and have a brand new teacher too.
I'll learn my new class rules
and what I'm supposed to do.

I hope I see my old teacher
to show how much I've grown.
I'll tell her all I did this summer
and how the time has flown.

I'm excited to go back to school
how ever will I sleep.
I'll read a book,
close my eyes, and
count blessings and sheep.

Back to school is coming soon,
so let's all give a cheer.
There is so much to look forward to
this exciting time of year!

www.ingramcontent.com/pod-product-compliance
Lightning Source LLC
Chambersburg PA
CBHW040316100426
42811CB00012B/1460